DEREK RERK

W9-ABD-112

The Me
Nobody Knew

The Me Nobody Knew

One particular morning felt weird. After a night of smokes and drinks, I woke up to see the sun slipping through the tear in the window shade, the woozy effects of Bud Dry still pooling in my head. The stereo was scratching some Iron Maiden song— something about killing the dead. *Lord, I hate that obnoxious rattle....*

I peeped out the window. Sunlight was reflecting off a fountain of water shooting from the sprinkler. A rush of energy swept through me. *I want to go home*, I thought. *I want to toss all my clothes in the wash, take a long shower, tie on a bathing suit, and lay out in the sun. I want to pour myself a glass of lemonade and feel normal again.*

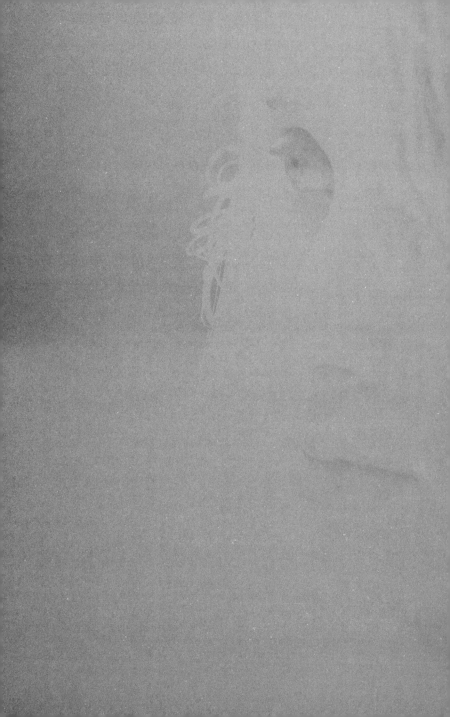

The Me
Nobody Knew

Shannon McLinden

revised edition

Carolrhoda Books   Minneapolis • New York

The images in this book are used with the permission of: © Adam Weiss/
Stone/Getty Images (teenager); © Caspar Benson/Getty Images (headlights).

Copyright © 2010 by Shannon McLinden

All rights reserved. International copyright secured. No part of this book may
be reproduced, stored in a retrieval system, or transmitted in any form or by
any means—electronic, mechanical, photocopying, recording, or otherwise—
without the prior written permission of Lerner Publishing Group, Inc., except
for the inclusion of brief quotations in an acknowledged review.

Carolrhoda Books
An imprint of Lerner Publishing Group, Inc.
241 First Avenue North
Minneapolis, MN 55401 U.S.A.

Website address: www.lernerbooks.com

Library of Congress Cataloging-In-Publication Data

McLinden, Shannon.
    The me nobody knew / by Shannon McLinden. — Rev. ed.
        p.   cm.
    Summary: The author describes her struggles with depression, concerns
about family, friends, dating, body image, and the difficulties of being a
teenage girl.
    ISBN: 978-0-7613-6384-2 (pbk. : alk. paper)
    1. McLinden, Shannon—Juvenile literature. 2. Teenage girls—
Minnesota—Coon Rapids—Biography—Juvenile literature. 3. Self-esteem
in adolescence—Minnesota—Coon Rapids—Juvenile literature. 4.
Self-esteem in women—Minnesota—Coon Rapids—Juvenile literature.
5. Achievement motivation in adolescence—Minnesota—Coon Rapids—
Juvenile literature. 6. Adolescent psychology—Minnesota—Coon
Rapids—Juvenile literature. I. Title.
HQ798.M437A3 2010
155.5'33092—dc22 [B]   2009040936

Manufactured in the United States of America
1 – BP – 12/15/2009

Dedication

To Pam Zimba, my favorite teacher. Thank you for opening the doors of your classroom to let me brighten the lives of your students. You have definitely brightened my life with your guidance and overwhelming kindness.

To my mom, dad, and brother, for your understanding. You have been wonderful in supporting me in sharing my joys and triumphs with the world. I love you very much.

To all of my friends, who laughed and cried with me through the years and who are at the heart of this book. Thank you for letting our mistakes become something all girls can learn from.

To my editor, Sara Saetre. You brought this to life! Thank you for capturing the real me in these pages.

To Tracy Williams and Hani Abu-Eideh.
You are two of the most amazing people I know. Thank you to my close friends Kerri Rieger, Amy Godlewski, and Jason Pruismann. You helped me greatly from start to finish.

To every girl who attended my workshops.
Thank you for validating my vision for this book.

You can read more about girls' issues, talk to Shannon McLinden, or connect with other girls at Shannon McLinden's website address: www.allaboutus.com.

I have great respect for every one of you reading this book. No one knows exactly what your life is like. Contrary to what most adults around you may believe, I'm sure parts of it aren't quite like Disneyland.

Life for me in middle school was difficult. Suicide crossed my mind often. Most of my friends talked about ending their lives. Some of us attempted. Finally one of the greatest people, one of my oldest friends, succeeded— and in succeeding, failed.

I have come a long way from the days when I wanted to die. It took me years to screw up as much as I did and learn from it. What I learned—what brought me back to life—is what you hold in your hands. Your fingers smooth its pages as you turn to discover what took me so long to find and deliver to you.

I changed some of the names in this book— of people, and of places. My own name is real. And this is my true story. I give it to you.

—*Shannon McLinden*

tell me
what you can

tell me not to worry
tell me not to cry
tell me joy won't go away
promise dreams don't die.

tell me that I'm pretty
tell me not to frown
tell me I'm not ugly
promise I can stand my ground.

tell me that I can
tell me that I should
tell me to always stand
promise you knew I could.

tell me death won't live
tell me life won't die
tell me to take what I give
promise you'll teach me to try.

tell me where my future ends
tell me of later plans
tell me where the road bends
promise to tell me what you can.

—*Shannon McLinden, a plea from the 12-year-old me*
to the 21-year-old me I thought I would never become

chapter one
don't want to die

We just get tired, or we get reborn, when we have suffered so much that we have started to die.

—Marianne Williamson, *A Return to Love*

I understood this for the first time at the end of eighth grade. I had been depressed for over a year. I mean, I had been sad before, but this was sadness somehow transformed. Instead of saving my tears for tremendous events like a fight with a friend, I cried over everything. I cried every morning as I put together an outfit to wear, I cried as I went down to the kitchen table, and I cried as I shoveled Fruity Pebbles into my mouth.

Then suddenly, and for a very long while, my emotions bottomed out. No more tears came. I just felt empty. I stared at walls, not really thinking about much at all. I was really tired all the time, like a flu virus had set in and decided to stay.

People would ask me, "What's wrong?"

"Nothing," I'd say.

I should have said, "Everything. I'm depressed."

Although the word *depressed* doesn't quite wrap up how I felt. I don't think there are words for that. My feelings were more like a long moan with jumbles of letters thrown in here and there. *UUUhhpffftgguuuughstfmoh*. Yeah, that's better.

The world seemed gray that summer, even as I lounged in my bikini on the deck behind my house, sweat pooling in my belly button from the heat of the midday sun. It was sunny, yes. But I don't remember feeling the sunshine soak through my pores, enticing me to call a friend to come over and laugh wildly with me and run through the sprinklers in the yard. No sun shone in my life.

My girlfriends were sort of aware of how I felt. But like most girls our age, they didn't seem to want anyone but themselves to get attention. Rather than sympathize with me, they shrugged me off and kept the attention on themselves. School was the same old joke day after day. More often than not, I sat on the bus alone. Dina was mad at me for flirting with Steve in history. Kathie was having a slumber party, and only five girls were invited. I wasn't one of them. Aimee gossiped about me every chance she got.

Girls are vicious. If one girl is upset and jealous, you can bet 10 more will join the bandwagon by the end of the day. There were more female fights than male fights at my school. And these were not so-called catfights. One girl was usually wearing brass knuckles, and the two girls would just beat the hell out of each other. I could have sworn I'd get an ulcer from worrying about whether I'd get beat up.

I always had a crush on someone new, and he always had a crush on one of the same three girls that every other boy at school had a crush on. I was the "good friend" of those girls, which meant I was always the girl in the background. Mike, the most beautiful guy in the world, would never see me as more than a friend.

My parents didn't know I had hit rock bottom; I didn't talk to them too much. Actually, I tried to avoid ever crossing their paths. All they thought was that my choice in clothes was a little boring. I dressed in dark clothes every day. Black. Navy.

"Why don't you wear something bright today?" my mom would ask.

"Because black is slimming," I'd say. Really, black reflected the black thoughts pooling in my head.

My brother, Scott, wasn't aware of my sadness either. He was three years older than me, and too absorbed in his hurried, happening, high-school life to notice that I had stopped smiling. Boy, was I lonely.

My family was sort of like that old TV show *Leave It to Beaver*. My parents had been 28 years old when they'd gotten married, and since then, they'd always been in love. Scott and I were definitely born into the "perfect" environment.

When we were little, Scott and I walked around holding hands. We built forts together out of couch cushions. We took turns playing Atari (the first video game, before Sega). Yes, he once put me in a box and threw me down a flight of stairs (always experiment on your sibling, right?). But most of the time, we were the best of friends.

My dad worked in government. Years ago, when we lived on the East Coast, our family helped out with a number of political campaigns. I remember climbing into a convertible, waving to crowds lining the streets, and throwing out heaps of candy.

My mom hosted parties—the kind that brought people together from all over the place. The guests laughed, talked, and listened to music until early in the morning. There were men in fitted black suits; their wives wore bright, expensive dresses and heavy perfume. I was passed from one knee to the next. "Hi little one! Aren't you just adorable!" I loved the attention. I heard people asking my parents, "What more could you want from your children? They are every parent's dream."

My brother and I volunteered for everything in our classes. We led the games after school in our neighborhood. Afterward, the kids came to our house, and my mom fed everybody. Scott and I didn't have a curfew, but we were always home by a decent time. We didn't have a list of chores to do, either, but we helped out when we could (my mom might disagree with this). We didn't often ask for things we knew we shouldn't get.

Then everything seemed to change overnight. One morning I woke up, looked at my mom, and thought, *Ugh. I don't want to talk to her. She is going to bug the heck out of me.* Soon I was calling my mom a "total wench." My dad was a "controlling jerk." After insulting them, I would say my mom "never cared about me" and my dad "never talked to me. He wasn't part of my life." There was always a different story for my anger. A lot of times the story didn't make sense. The bottom line was, I always said I hated them.

My parents were typical, extraordinary parents—fixing me breakfast, leaving spending money for me on the kitchen table, helping me with my homework after they got home from work. But their kindness bothered me so much. I wanted scrambled eggs, but I didn't want my mom to make them. I could do it *myself*. And why did they have to offer to help me study for history? Did I look like I needed help? I was smart. I could study *alone*. I thought I could manage everything alone, even this never-ending case of the blues.

Looking back, I can't figure out how all the little parts of my life that I hated could outweigh the bigger parts that I liked. I had plenty going for me. I was an A student. I was popular, even president of my class. Over the years I threw fun, clean parties, where my mom made tables of food and my dad joined the guys on the couch watching basketball. Every group came, converged, and mingled in my family room. It was really something to see. For those few hours, we climbed out of our thick shells and made friends with everyone and anyone.

But those few hours were just a memory when the school bell rang Monday morning. It was the same routine, day after day. Walk in. Go to my locker. Be told "I love your hair!" by the same group of girls who yesterday talked behind my back. (This morning, of course, I was their best friend again.) It didn't matter that I was smart and outgoing, that I had a caring family. I could never be as pretty as the rest of them, or as skinny or as cool.

I didn't like myself. I had naturally curly brown hair. Apparently it was every girl's dream, but it wasn't mine. Mine was to have fine blonde hair so long and straight it would drape over my shoulders in a sheen of silk like the model's hair in the Pantene commercials. Blonde hair would have been perfect to go with my blue eyes. Blonde hair—blue eyes. A package deal. Unfortunately, the only package I had was a head of short curls and a face of freckles. "Cute," people called me. But I wanted to be beautiful.

And I wanted to be skinny. I weighed 80-some pounds, but it didn't matter. No one ever said I was "skinny." When I sat with my legs crossed, I would glance down and see what I thought was blubber. My thighs were chubby, so my pants never fit right. I shopped for jeans at every store imaginable, but I looked like I had huge hips in every pair. I just thought, *I'm unbelievably fat.*

I tried a new diet every month. I'd eat just meat, or no meat; just Slim Fast bars; just salad; or just about nothing. I had no energy and a growing obsession with measuring how close my inner thighs came to touching as I stood, feet together, in front of a mirror.

It was all the fine details (that only I seemed to see) that bothered me the most: dimples, shadows, freckles, folds of skin, weird-shaped toenails. My smile was crooked; my body wasn't tan enough.

Whenever anyone looked at me, I tried not to make eye contact. If I did, the results were devastating. I just knew they were staring at my ugly face or my screwed-up hair. I was numb. There was a black, hollow mass behind my eyes. *UUUhhpffftggguuuughstfmoh.*

The only peace I found was late at night. Sometimes, after my parents were asleep, I would ever so quietly slip out the back door of my house. Still wearing my pajamas, I'd walk about 10 houses up the street to the neighborhood park. My dad surely would have lectured me if he had known of my secret hikes because of what he called "potential dangers."

"But this is Coon Rapids, Minnesota," I'd tell him, "and the only potential dangers in this pretty, little green suburb are being attacked by swarms of mosquitoes and being escorted home by the curfew police." (I swear Coon Rapids was the only city in the country where police actually enforced a stupid "10-o'clock-on-school-nights" rule.)

Anyway, I would follow the winding path in the park through the trees to the playground, where I would sit on a swing, feeling the dampness from the seat seep through my pajamas to my goose-bumped legs. For hours, I'd gaze steadily out across the field of grass before me, wondering why peace like this never lingered around when the sun rose in the morning.

On mornings after nights like these, I would wake in a sleepy haze, wanting nothing more than to shut my eyes forever and find the peace I'd experienced the night before. Days went by in such a muted blur that sometimes I felt like I hadn't actually existed the day before. Not even the funniest stand-up comic could make me laugh. In fact, not even a really good song from an awesome movie—a song that had made me jump up, wave my arms in the air, and sing into an imaginary microphone before—could brighten my day. My limbs turned down the request for a dance, and my adrenaline decided to take the day off.

Things all around just never seemed to go my way. And every one of those things piled in my mind like junk stuffed in a closet, just waiting for the door to open so it could tumble out in a ferocious wave.

Alcohol made it easier for me to talk to people about my feelings. Starting in seventh grade, my friends and I would sneak liquor out of our parents' wine cabinets and bring it in hair spray bottles to our slumber parties. Someone would always pull out cigarettes, and we smoked and drank and talked about who the good-looking boys were. Eventually, we'd all pass out on the floor.

The next morning, we'd go home and stash our hair spray bottles in secret places. I just put mine with the rest of my hair junk in my room, because my parents knew I hated them to come near my room anyway. I always had one last thing to remember: I had to wash my clothes as soon as possible. If my mom smelled the smoke on my shirt, I was dead.

I wrote poems about my life every night, and I kept a journal. On those nights when the junk in my mind started to push at the door's hinges, I wrote about wanting to die and end it all. I fantasized about my friends walking into my room and finding me dead on the floor, pills scattered across the rug, an empty bottle clutched in my hand. I definitely wanted a dramatic effect.

Then one night my friend Lisa had a party. Her parents were out of town, her aunt bought us a keg, and half the kids in our grade showed up. Of course I went. Lisa was one of my best friends, most days. And anyway, if you didn't go to a party like that one, you might start losing your reputation with the party-hard crowd. You had to go.

Well, that particular night I drank 13 beers. In an hour I went from a sober, sane, social butterfly to a drunken, crying, lonesome mess huddled in a corner of the upstairs bathroom.

(Oh, what great things alcohol will do for you.) I was crying so hard that I was sporadically gasping for air and dry-heaving over the toilet.

I closed my eyes tightly, wishing over and over that I could feel normal again. *Why is my life so hard*, I wondered. *I'm pretty good looking, smart, outgoing, even funny sometimes. I know I am all these things, but I don't feel like I'm any of them. I hate coming to these stupid parties. I hate my ugly body, my screwed-up hair, the backstabbing among my girlfriends. I hate this, I hate this, I hate this. I don't want to live this life anymore.*

I stood up and staggered to the bathroom door, seeing nothing but a foggy blur. I made my way through the loud party in the kitchen and out the door. I stumbled down the driveway, down toward the dark, busy street.

I was so tired. My stomach hurt from throwing up, my eyes were swollen and red, my legs wobbled from the alcohol. Worst of all, my head hurt from thinking so long and so hard about how much I hated myself and my far-from-perfect life. In the darkness, I could see headlights speeding toward me.

My closet of crap was full. The door burst open, the junk tumbled out, and the ferocious wave swept me with it into the street. I gave up hoping. Blinded, I stepped off the curb, into the path of that fast-moving car.

Suddenly, I felt myself wrenched backwards and up. I was folding in half and landing, not on the car, but on the shoulder of Zach Conway, one of the cutest boys in my class. He had pulled me to safety. Zach was screaming, "Shannon, are you freaking nuts?"

Like a four-year-old girl clinging to her daddy, arms locked firmly around his neck, I just held on tight to Zach. I was so scared—of myself, of having crossed the line to a point where I no longer merely contemplated death, but instead leaped right in front of it. *Yes*, I thought, *I must be nuts.*

In that moment, with cars whisking by on the dark street behind us, a flicker of faith ignited in the hollowness within me. I said to Zach, "Don't put me down. I don't want to die."

Yes, it is true. When we have suffered so much, we have started to die. We just get tired, so tired. And as I learned—we are reborn.

chapter two
don't want what i've got

Why couldn't I have been born male? Males have it easy, don't they? They don't have to wear makeup. They don't even have that option. Their clothes don't have to be tight to be flattering. They can belch, fart, sneeze, blow their noses (with notebook paper), and sweat buckets in a T-shirt they've worn for over a week without washing it. And girls will still love them.

It is true: Most of us at some time find ourselves attracted to no-mannered, nonshowering, foul-mouthed, or uncaring guys. What is the deal? I was always attracted to these types. After one relationship (if you can call it that) would end, and after all the hurt in me cried itself out, I'd vow never to date a boy again. Until a week later, when I'd meet another schmuck or maybe just get back together with the same old jerk. So there I was, back in the game, desperate to win the heart of a guy who didn't deserve it in the first place, trying everything except being who I really was. It is amazing what we girls will do to ourselves.

I spotted Matt at the start of my ninth grade year. He was a year younger than me, had a naturally dark complexion and chocolate-brown hair. He wore baggy jeans and big sweaters and never really matched his clothes. He was what my friends and I called a "hottie." Hotties were guys who didn't have their act together. You know— they weren't very classy. But boy, were they good looking. Like Andy, who had shoulder-length blond hair, wore a black leather jacket, and smoked Marlboros. Or John, who had a baby face, great abs, and cheesy pickup lines.

A hottie would date one of our friends for a month, break up, and move on to another friend. Hotties all used the same lines, like, "I feel like I could tell you anything. You changed my life from the minute I saw you by your locker." What a joke! We knew these guys weren't the best for us, but I guess we thought that having somebody to love is better than having no one. Most of the hotties never got far enough down their dating list to get to me. I should have felt lucky. Instead I just felt lonely—until Matt arrived.

Matt wasn't smart, or polite, or mature (what was I thinking?). I saw him get kicked out of class several times. I also saw him coming down on younger kids, dumping their books in the hallways and laughing at them. Matt was rebellious and mysterious. Call me crazy, but I thought I was in love.

I spent countless hours decorating the knees of my jeans with "I Love Matt" doodles. My homework, notes to friends, and even my hands displayed my undying love. I was so excited to see him every day, especially fourth hour. I had geometry; he had some class—I don't remember what—next door. A suspended divider separated my class from his. By bending down, I could see his neon green shoelaces dangling from his soccer shoes. Those shoelaces drove me crazy. Geometry? Ha! With fluorescent green flashing before my eyes, I wasn't going to try to figure out the length of side A of a triangle. All I cared about was the length of the floor between me and him—the distance that kept him just beyond my reach, next door.

Anyway, a friend of mine told a friend of his that I liked him. Somehow (the details are fuzzy here) Matt and I ended up walking back to his house after school and kissing in his bedroom (that part isn't so fuzzy). Within the next couple of days, Matt gave me his big, gray sweater, four times too big for me. He also gave me his red high-top shoes. They were size nine—more than twice my size. He told me to wear this stuff.

Anything for Matt. I wanted to do everything I could to get him to love me, even if I had to look like a clown, literally. As I clunked through the halls in those huge shoes, all I could think was *I feel owned. I love this.*

Matt gave me a lot of attention, and I felt important. Even if the attention was not positive. Even if it was mean—and sometimes it was. His friends would come out of gym class wired with energy, and they'd head straight for my locker. One at a time, they'd bump into me. Someone would brush my arm. Another would tip my books. Once a kid kicked my foot. All of them laughed, even Matt. Then he just shrugged his shoulders and said, "See ya!"

Two of my male friends, Zach and Tim, thought I had lost my mind. They hated the guy. They didn't like the way he treated me. And Matt was younger. He wasn't in our group, he wasn't an athlete, and he wore neon green shoelaces. Boy, did Zach and Tim want to beat him up.

Well, their day came. As usual, Matt and his friends were joking around by my locker one morning. One of the guys threw Matt into me. The group pushed against both of us, pinning me against the door of my locker. They all laughed, including Matt. Zach and Tim saw this. They rushed over, picked Matt up by his shirt, threw him against the wall, and dumped his books. They told him, "Don't ever come near Shannon again."

I felt like I was in a movie. My heroes had saved me (heroes I would later date, but that's off the subject). Over the next couple of days, whenever Matt called my house, I always hung up on him. Whenever he came by my locker, I walked away. And that was the end of Matt.

Why is it we feel like we are nothing without a boy in our lives? Even after Matt, I still thought I needed to change myself to be loved. Meanwhile, all the good-looking, popular guys (the ones we draw hearts around in our yearbooks) always go for the same two or three beautiful girls. Even each guy in a group of friends will take a turn dating and dumping the same girl. Same group of guys. Same girl. Same story every time.

Take Mike for example. He was so good looking, and so conceited. He dated and dumped some of my best friends. And I waited for four years to date him! He never gave me the time of day.

My three friends in the limelight—Lisa, Julie, and Domenica—were the three girls all the guys had a crush on. They were beautiful, every guy's dream. And the models in the magazines I read—like *Seventeen*—were so beautiful. Everything about me looked wrong. I wanted it all to change.

Rummaging through my closet for hours each night, I would frantically look for an outfit to wear the next day. If I couldn't find something cute, my day would be ruined. If my hair didn't turn out when I fixed it before school—if it was flat, frizzy, or sticking up—I considered staying home.

Makeup helped me feel prettier. I used eye shadow and black eyeliner to make my big blue eyes look brighter. I wore the latest lipstick shade. With foundation, I could cover my pimples and make my face look tanner.

Tan! I went to tanning beds. At one point, I was so addicted to tanning beds that if I missed a day, I was sure I looked ghost-white. In reality, I was as dark as a tree. My skin looked like leather. I'm sure it actually was turning into leather from the UV rays. I was so obsessed.

What I wanted was to look exactly like Lisa, Julie, or Domenica. Lisa was on dance line. She looked like a Broadway star when she plastered on her stage makeup and slipped into her itty-bitty, sequined outfit. She looked beautiful all made up. She looked even more beautiful after softball practice when she had dirt on her face and wore her cap backwards over her long, shiny brown hair. I swear, she could have quit showering and wearing deodorant. Males still would have flocked to her, thinking her smell was a wonderful, new cologne.

Oh, I remember sitting in the stands during athletic events when the dance line came out. When a certain part of the girls' dance came up—the part where they turned their backs to the crowd, and their little twirly skirts flew in the air as they bent forward to the ground—every male in the audience moaned with excitement. Particularly because Lisa was in front.

Julie was Lisa's best friend. Julie had brown hair, too, and she was also on dance line. Julie and Lisa were both skinny. And Julie looked just as great as Lisa after softball. Now that I think about it, they were almost identical. Together, they were funny enough to make a table of guys laugh, courageous enough to pick a fight with another girl, and cool enough that when they came to school in men's boxer shorts and T-shirts, every girl at school had the same outfit on the next day. It happened.

Domenica had blazing red hair, a tan complexion, and big boobs. I don't feel bad saying it. She did, and we all knew it. The guys loved it. I say this because I distinctly remember an afternoon when about 10 of us went swimming in Zach's pool. As Domenica took off her shirt to jump in, the guys moaned with excitement. One of them chimed in with a below-the-border, Cheech 'n' Chong voice, "God, I love America."

I wanted the boys who liked Lisa, Julie, and Domenica to like me, too. I can remember dressing similar to those girls. I bought the same CoverGirl foundation they used, the same Wet 'n' Wild "Pink Ice" lipstick. Everything they did, I did too. I tried to laugh like them, pushing my hand out in front of me and tossing my head back with an outrageous, eye-drawing laugh.

For a while, I really thought my plan was going to work. I'd look and feel just like them. But I never got more than a temporary feeling of "okayness." Soon I was down and dragging again, slipping toward the place I'd been the night when Zach had saved me.

One day after school, my mom drove me to Northtown Mall so I could find a new dress to wear to the choir concert the following week. It was a big to-do because it was our ninth grade year, and one of the final big concerts we would sing before leaving middle school for high school. I had to wear something new. This time, I thought I'd follow my sunnier heart, venture from black, and try something with color. I found a short, peach-colored, silk tank dress at one store. Thrilled, I stepped into the dressing room to try it on.

When I looked in the mirror, I just bawled. *If I was a guy, and I didn't know me, I'd say I am butt-ugly. My thighs touch; my arms bulge; my hips are huge. I should be the "before" picture on a Weight Watchers commercial.* Since I weighed about 87 pounds, I doubt I could have passed for a "before" picture. But that's how I felt. I took the dress off as quickly as I could and climbed back into the big, bulky black clothes I wore to hide my fat body. I wouldn't be buying anything that day.

When we got home, I told my mom that I felt terrible and that I needed someone to help me feel better. You know moms. She asked, "Why? Maybe I can help. You know sometimes I feel bad, too. But then I come around. . . ."

"No, Mom. No. No. No," I told her. "Standing here right now, knowing what I look like and who I am, I can honestly say I would rather be dead." I definitely was not subtle. She immediately rummaged through the phone book, called a psychologist, and made an appointment for me.

What an experience! First I had to take a self-esteem test. When the test was scored, a doctor came in and told my mom and me, "Shannon is depressed." *No! Really? What a genius! You know, I never thought depression had anything to do with my wanting to die.*

I finally met my psychologist, Laura. Hated her. What a fake person. "Oh *hiieey*! How are *youuuu*! Sit down here on this fluffy little couch. Go ahead and hold my little stuffed bear, George. This is your own special little place. Make yourself at home." Puke. I kept thinking, *She needs to take her little self and get a little life.* I wanted to get out of the lady's office. She talked to me like I was wearing a pink bonnet on my head, sucking a bottle, and fastened in a diaper. What a quack!

I only met with her three times over a month. All she did was listen as I carried on about my problems. After she listened, she told me a jumble of things I could do to feel better, like movies I could watch and books I could read. *Like reading a nice little book will solve my problems.* She pointed out people I should stay away from (competitive, rat-race friends and people who put me down). *It's not that easy to "just stay away" from friends. They're all I've got.* A world existed in which I could find peace, said Laura the psychologist. *If it was out there, I was light-years away from it.* Finding that world would not be easy, though.

I could not fall fool to any "quick fix." The trick was that I needed to create that peaceful world on my own. To do this, I would need to relearn what it means to be a girl.

chapter three
the friendship factor

It's hard to say where my reputation sat on that spectrum spanning from geeks to head-bangers to freaks. I had friends in all different groups. I guess I was what I would call a floater, moving from one clique to the next. But from lots of my friends I'd hear, "Why are you friends with *them*?" "Them," I guess, referred to the popular group—the stick-tight, head-up, party-hard girls and boys who were always getting into something devious, something new. And yes, I was part of that group, too.

It was tough being a floater. I had to change myself depending on who I was with. If I was with the wild crowd, I joined the swearing and complaining about schoolwork. When tests were graded and passed back in class, I faked a reaction to avoid being called a nerd. "Oh, my parents are going to kill me!" I moaned, sliding my A+ into a folder. But if I was sitting with my study group in

English class, I became quiet, conservative, and focused on "making the grade." When I ate with some of the guys at lunch, I would pull my shoulders back, flip my hair, and try to talk guy-talk with an added sexy flare. Yes, I could fit in everywhere. Yet really I fit in nowhere, because I could never be the real me.

I liked everybody and everybody seemed to like me. *Seemed* is the important word here, though, because you never knew, when your back was turned, what opinions would be rudely whispered about you.

Aimee was one of the people always doing the whispering. She wanted compliments flowing in her direction only. Once I showed up in class with a new shirt on, and someone said, "Your shirt is cool!" Aimee leaned to a friend next to her and whispered, "I saw Tina wearing that shirt last week. She looked a lot better in it, you know?" Soon her opinion filtered through the minds of everybody else. *It never fails*, I thought. *I just can't win.*

I had so many ways to count the number of my friends. I counted how many people stood in a cluster around my locker to gossip before school started, how many friends sat with me at lunch, how many notes I dumped on my desk at the end of the school day, how many phone calls I got in one night.

To me, those numbers were the measure of my friends. And boy, the numbers always changed, and I noticed. If Nikki gave me a bad look, if she didn't smile when I said hi to her, my stomach turned. That very hour I had to write her a note and ask her what the bad look was for. Usually I found out what was bothering her long before the note ever got to her.

"Shannon," somebody would tell me with a bucket of sarcasm, "Kari and Jill saw Nikki stare you down this morning. They said you said Nikki kissed Scott last week, and Nikki is pissed. She said Scott said not to tell anyone and she told you because she thought you wouldn't tell anyone and you did and now Scott is mad and his girlfriend found out and now she's mad at Nikki so Nikki said she is going to kick your ass."

Did you understand that? Neither did I. What a freaking mess. No wonder I was a basket case.

If my phone didn't ring one night, or if I called someone and left a message and they didn't call me back, I felt completely alone. If I received a note from someone (this is *the worst*) that said, "So-and-so heard what you said about her and now Lisa, Angela, Melody, Alyssa, and Danielle are mad at you," I knew I was doomed.

Every day was a different circus. On days when everything seemed to go right (my pockets were stuffed with notes, my phone rang, girls hung out), I felt like I was on top of the world. On days when everything seemed to go sour (friends talked behind my back, my hair wouldn't work right, my face broke out), I went home and cried.

For a long time I had so many friends that I couldn't even count them. Yet I'd never been so lonely or confused. I envied people who were shy or quiet, who were kind of middle-school wallflowers. They were so removed from the action—the "fit-in-or-get-out" action—that to them middle school was just like summer camp. Lord, I wish it had felt like that for me.

Thank goodness for Amy. Amy was the first person I met when I moved to Minnesota in the second grade. We met during show-and-tell. I stood up with at least 13 little pink and yellow barrettes clamped on 13 clumps of hair I had randomly chosen. I showed the class pictures of the house we'd lived in. Then Amy stood up with her dirty-blonde hair hanging down to her butt, bangs falling an inch over her eyes. She told the class about the 7 poodles her family owned. She really wanted one of my barrettes. Come to find out, Amy lived in my neighborhood. We walked home together and watched TV at my house. Every day after that we did the same thing.

In third grade once, Amy and I rode our bikes around a big dump site near our homes. We rummaged through the junk, and I found a box filled with rocks. Some of the rocks were split in half; they had purple and white crystals inside. Of course we carried the box home. Two weeks later, there was a rock show at Northtown Mall. Amy and I took our box over there to see if the rock people could identify our rocks. Identify them? They bought them! We got $25 each. We bought brand-new Strawberry Shortcake dolls with the money.

We shared everything—clothes, lockers, hair spray, even the same tent when we pretended to camp in her backyard. When I wanted to build a tree house, Amy never questioned why. She just came over with a hammer and nails. Which doesn't mean we were always perfect friends. There were lots of less-than-perfect days. I accidentally slammed her fingers in the door to my house one day. She accidentally closed a van door on my hand. Another time, she dumped a bowl of spaghetti on my head. I threw Jello-O back at her. We kept even.

Another time when we were in grade school, we put on our bathing suits and tried an experiment. I have no idea how we heard to try this, but we filled the tub with an inch of water, then poured at least 20 different kinds of soap into it: shampoo, dish soap, laundry detergent, liquid hand soap, and bubble bath. We sat in the tub and rotated our arms to churn up bubbles. Our spinning arms reminded me of the way we'd once turned our bicycles upside down and spun the pedals, pretending to make popcorn.

In two minutes, we had enough bubbles to bury us. Bubbles overflowed the tub and swept across the bathroom floor in a froth two feet deep. It was awesome. We got out of the tub and ran and slid around the floor on our butts, losing ourselves in the bubbles. They felt like whipped cream.

After hours of slipping and sliding, our hair matted with bubbles, our butts sore from sliding, we knew we had to quit. My parents would be home soon, and we had to get rid of the bubbles. We started carrying armfuls of bubbles out to the backyard, throwing them to the winds. By the time we were done, the yard was full of glistening clouds. We danced around like angels.

Amy never hung around any of my other friends in middle school. She hated to be a part of the treadmill we were on, always trying to be cool. I began learning the true measure of friendship with Amy, and it looked a lot like heaven.

chapter four
home alone

I remember stepping off the bus after school in ninth grade, thrilled to be done for the day. I'd throw a sandwich together or eat a bowl of cereal. Then I'd turn on the TV and collapse on the couch in total ecstasy. My brother, Scott, was never around. Days when Amy didn't come home with me, it was just me, my remote, and MTV.

By 5:30, the garage door would open. My father's car would pull in. My stomach turned. I didn't want to talk to him. It didn't matter if I had been laughing at the funniest show on TV—I wouldn't laugh when my dad was around. I didn't want him to see me smile. When he asked, "How was school?" I mumbled, expressionless, "Fine."

"I can't hear you. What did you say?" he'd ask.

Of course you couldn't hear me. I did that on purpose. "Fine!" I'd scream. Then I'd get up off the couch, stomp to my room, and slam the door.

My reaction to my dad was nothing compared to my fury when my mom talked to me. Just hearing her voice made so much anger grow inside me that my face got flushed and I just became infuriated. I don't think I could carry on a normal conversation with her. I was always trying so hard to ignore her. Sometimes I almost whispered when I had to speak to her. Other times I'd whine, or sound frustrated and angry.

"Shannon," she said one day, "we've decided that the four of us are going to take a little vacation at Wisconsin Dells this weekend. Ask Amy if she wants to come too. She likes roller coasters, doesn't she?"

Immediately I jumped in. "Why would Amy want to come? Do I have to go? Why does the whole family have to go? You know, I have a life." I started to scream. "You never let me do what I want to do. You're always telling me what to do! Screw this vacation! Screw you!"

As the words built in my stomach, flooded up, and rolled off my tongue, relief began to soothe me. *I love to yell like this. What a relief to speak my mind.*

Now, you should know that my parents had never fought in front of my brother and me. I don't think they ever raised their voices to each other. Whenever Scott or I did something wrong (like egging somebody's house), my parents sat us down for a family meeting. My father would begin. "Children," he'd say. "What were you thinking? Do you understand. . . ? "

Whatever the problem, my parents made us talk it through. Carefully. Then my father would say, "Have we learned from this?" I knew they felt hurt when I ignored them or screamed at them. I could see it in their eyes. I really liked to see them upset. Upsetting them felt like revenge. Revenge for what? I don't know.

It's funny. My friends thought my parents were the best. They'd say, "Shannon, your mom and dad are so cool. I'd give anything to have them."

I'd always have an excuse. "You just don't understand," I'd say. They didn't. Sometimes I exaggerated when I told my friends about little arguments I had with my parents so my mom and dad would look like the bad guys. My friends never believed me.

One day I decided I could really hurt my parents by just never being around. I started a new routine. I would stop at home after school and write a note, telling my parents where I would be. Then I'd go to a friend's house. At about nine o'clock I'd come home and walk right downstairs, into my bedroom.

"Why don't you tell us how school was, Shannon?" my parents would ask.

"I have nothing to tell you," I'd say, and shut my door.

On top of not being around, I completely cleaned out my room. I took all the posters off my wall. I stuffed my clothes into drawers and the closet. I put my stereo and alarm clock under the bed. I stashed all my makeup and hair spray in a bag that I took to school. My room looked like a den. *Maybe if I make it seem like I'm actually not living here anymore, they'll realize how nice it was to have me around in the first place.*

I kept up my antics of not speaking to my parents for over a month. Then one day, my mom came downstairs to my room and knocked. She looked like she was going to cry. "I can't stand this any longer, Shannon," she said. "What's wrong? It's like you aren't even our daughter anymore."

I said nothing. She closed the door. Honestly, right then, I couldn't picture myself living past the age of 16. Not only couldn't I picture it, I didn't want to. Where was my life going to go? *If the rest of my life is this depressing, please let it be short.* Then I lay back on my bed and cried myself to sleep.

Days after nights like that, sometimes Amy and I would skip school. We would get to school, walk through the front doors, and stop. We'd look around and say, "I don't feel like being here. Let's leave." Then we'd walk to my house and call our moms at work. We'd tell them we didn't feel well and they needed to call the school.

We weren't really lying. Amy and I skipped when we were depressed. We couldn't have concentrated anyway. How can you enjoy English when you don't enjoy waking up in the morning?

Sometimes after we got to my house, we'd watch movies all day. Other days we just cried for hours together about how sad we were. But we always ended up laughing, baking cookies, or painting pictures. For those few, brief times together, Amy and I felt happy just to be alive.

chapter five
bad crowds

A new girl came to school. It was all the talk. She was at least six inches taller than the biggest girl presently enrolled at West (we called it "Jail" Middle School). She was older—at least 17. Everybody thought she was so cool because of her age, but I thought she was stupid. What was a 17-year-old doing in middle school? She was either very behind on I.Q. points or very dangerous. Dangerous girls were always sent away for a while to Mill City Juvenile Detention Center. And obviously, Jenya was a survivor of Mill.

The detention center was like a parent's last hope, an extended vacation for their delinquent children. Most of the time, girls who were sent there would eventually come back telling "prison" survival stories about how they were beaten and forced to live on saltine crackers for weeks. They acted like they were legends. But Mill seemed like a hellish hole to most of us.

Jenya looked like one of those plastic windmill toys on a stick. She was tall and clanky. Apparently Mill never let her out of her cell to play in the yard, because her skin was so white, I swear you could see right through her. If you blew wind her way—a glance, a nod, or even a smile—she let loose. "What the hell are you looking at? You wanna die, you little prick?"

She was really pleasant, as you can tell.

I couldn't say a word to that girl back then. I couldn't look at her. I was afraid to stand by her because if she happened to not like the looks of someone hanging around, she would ask you, "Who the hell are you and what makes you think I want you standing next to me?" She had a habit of beating people up for no reason.

Well, Jenya and her loser crowd began to mix with some of my friends, and I had to follow their lead. Even my best friends liked her. Of course they did. We'd do anything not to get our asses kicked. It was just pathetic hearing them talk about her. "Have you met Jenya? Oh, she is *sooo* cool. She is 17, loves to party, and she's just out of Mill. She tried to stab someone or something—but she is so bad ass."

I think even my friends knew how stupid they sounded. But who cares? We had a rebel on our side.

Well, Jenya started loaning herself out to younger girls who needed someone to represent them in a fight. Most fights took place at the water tower across the street from school. Jenya would walk over there with the girl who needed help. They would wait for the girl who had picked a fight. When the girl showed up, Jenya would step up and spit in the girl's face. She'd say, "You picked a fight with one of my girls. You fight them—you fight me. Got that? No one screws with us."

No one did. Even when Jenya wasn't involved, the fight-picker usually backed down. Thank goodness. I was one of the fightees several times, and I specifically remember being so scared that I would have to step up to punch. I truly could have gone into shock. I would have frozen, panicked, or worse—just bawled my eyes out.

Some girls followed through with a fight, though. A crowd of us would dash to the water tower after the bell rang to watch. Sometimes one girl would give up. She'd cry, scream, and try to run. The winner would run after her, pull her by the hair, and throw her onto the ground, kicking her. If the loser tried to get up and run, the winner would start in on her all over again. We'd run along with the two, watching, laughing, cheering for a side. It was sick.

I particularly recall one time, seeing so much blood on this one poor girl. *How can I watch someone suffer like this and not try to stop the fight?* The scene seemed to move in slow motion, the sound blurred. As the crowd moved on with the fight, I stood still, feeling them push past me. And I threw up. Right there on the curb. *I deserve this. What kind of person have I become?*

Well, fighting was the least of our bad actions. Most of what my friends and I did was in secret. Parents had no idea. My friends were football players, cheerleaders, honor roll students. I was even voted student of the month! To most parents, we were all poster children for wholesomeness. But secretly, we were a bad crowd.

It's true, some other kids were worse. There were plenty of dropouts, hard-core lawbreakers, "juvie" junkies. But we had access to those people, and to the alcohol, acid, speed, and marijuana they always seemed to have around. We knew older losers, too—bar owners, and people who made or sold drugs.

We were the kind of kids that parents would have warned their kids against—had they known. We had the grades, the activities, and the charm that made us seem like the "good kids." At heart we were good kids. We just wanted to fit in. We wanted to be the best (which was usually the worst): the best drunk, the best fighter, the best partier.

I really got a taste of the bad crowd when I hung around Kim and Rena. Both of them were petite, pretty girls who were considered "total sweethearts." They were sweethearts, yes, but sweethearts with bad habits that we all shared.

Whenever Kim's mom was out of town, Kim, Rena, and I would go out and buy a box of Vivarin. Then we'd spend the night at Kim's, have a sort of slumber party. We would go to the house across the street from Kim's where some guys lived. I can remember one of the guys vividly. Kai had long, blond hair and a Metallica T-shirt. He always had a cigarette in his hand. He looked like he should be running a porno shop.

Well, Kai would take our money and buy us alcohol and cigarettes. Then he and his brothers and their friends would come over to Kim's. We would smoke and take Vivarin and drink. Take more Vivarin. Drink. I was scared of those guys. They were scummy, old, need-a-life guys who had nothing better to do than buy underage girls booze and then stay to hang out. Pathetic.

Every once in a while, Kai would come back with a little Glad baggy with tiny pieces of paper in it. He'd hand the baggy to Kim and Rena, who would put one of the microscopic squares on their tongues. Minutes later, they were hyper and dizzy. Sometimes they screamed or cried or described the colors and shapes and people they saw floating around the room.

Those times with Kim and Rena were the only times I saw someone on acid. I never tried it myself. Oddly enough, that was because I was deathly afraid of beetles. I just knew that if I tried any of that crap, I'd be seeing beetles crawl all over me. I'd go mad. It just didn't seem too appealing.

Once we all packed into the rusty green beater car Kai had been "working on" for years. *He needs a new hobby.* We drove to the annual Coon Rapids carnival. Trash city. Seriously. Nothing good ever came of going there. It is loserville. Well, at this carnival there was a double-wide trailer behind the game area. I always thought maybe the workers slept there or ate there or something.

As it turned out, that wasn't all they did there. Kim went into the trailer with some fat, trashy guy who needed to shave, shower, and brush his teeth. I kept thinking, *Why did she go with him? She is so stupid. She's going to get attacked. We're not going to be able to help. Lord! Why did we come here?* Twenty minutes later, Kim came out—smiling. She had a pocketful of speed. She'd watched this guy make it in his double-wide drug den. Getting the stuff was just too easy.

At school, fights were scheduled as usual. Every now and then someone got kicked out of class for making crude jokes, letting off fart bombs, or swearing at the teacher. Meanwhile, teachers never saw the guys and girls popping speed into their mouths like it was Luden's cough drops, or the people hanging out in the bathroom between classes, swigging from pocket-sized bottles of Jim Beam or smoking hand-rolled weed.

If I recall correctly, everything went wrong all at once. A rumor spread that a teacher had smelled alcohol on some kid's breath. The teacher sent the kid to the principal's office, and the police came and gave the kid a breath test. It was a rumor, but if it happened, the kid was burnt. We stopped bringing alcohol to our lockers from then on. We couldn't have brought it anyway, because school officials began checking lockers. They said they were checking to see if we were sharing lockers, but that was crap. They were looking for the dirty stuff.

That same week, my friend Tricia got off her bus and walked to her locker with a sort of glazed-over look in her eyes. She had her hands clasped behind her neck like she was stressed or something. When she dropped her hands out from under her long hair, we could see strips of blood-soaked gauze around her wrists, dangling where she'd unwrapped them. She fell to the ground, crying. We all knew Tricia's father hit her a lot and told her she was worthless. Still, we never thought she'd try to commit.

No one ever saw her again. We thought her dad probably packed up their belongings and moved to another city. I'm sure he blamed Tricia's problems on the school.

It was a dramatic and touching scene she made. But afterward, we all talked about how stupid it was that she tried to kill herself. Frankly, I think we were all upset because she hadn't come to us for help. If she had no concern for our feelings, we would have no concern for hers. We tried to forget about her.

But we were all hypocrites. Probably every one of us had thought about suicide or even tried it. And we had all imagined a big dramatic scene at the end like the one Tricia made. We'd have visitors at the hospital, cards, and phone calls. Reality is never what you hope it will be.

Not long after that, Kim, Rena, and I spent a Friday night at Kim's. After hours of drinking and smoking, we saw her mom pulling into the driveway. *She's not supposed to be back!* We stashed the Bud Dry. We left the cigarettes out, since Kim's mom was a smoker and actually offered us cigarettes sometimes. I called my mom and told her to come pick me up.

Not until my mom was waiting in the driveway did it occur to me that I smelled like a chimney. I ran to the kitchen and rinsed off my hands in the sink. I popped a few radishes in my mouth. Then I ran out and jumped in the car.

Mom was all over it. "Shannon, what is that awful smell?"

Oh sh—. "What smell?"

"Give me your hand." She grabbed my hand and smelled my fingers. She didn't say a word. She was letting the point sink in. What an ass

I'd made of myself. Nothing covers the smell of smoke on your clothes, in your hair, under your nails. And here I was, stuffing radishes down my throat, hoping my mom would think I smelled like a salad.

She was right. I reeked—of too much smoke, alcohol, anger, recklessness, dirt, lying, shame, and hurt. I knew the person inside me was better than this. And I knew I had better get the courage to change soon. I would start by getting out of the bad crowd.

chapter six
born again

Change doesn't happen overnight, and I still spent time at Kim's. One particular morning felt weird. After a night of smokes and drinks, I woke up to see the sun slipping through the tear in the window shade, the woozy effects of Bud Dry still pooling in my head. Stale, smoke-saturated air coated my throat like liquid cough syrup. *UUUhhpffftgguuuughstfmoh*.

I surveyed the room. A boy was crouched in a corner, snoring with his mouth open. Crushed beer cans were piled like a pillow behind him. Kim and Rena lay in sleeping bags on the floor, the heads of two boys propped on their legs. The stereo was scratching some Iron Maiden song— something about killing the dead. I sighed with complete mental exhaustion. *Lord, I hate that obnoxious rattle*.

I sat up. Leaning to my right, I strained to catch a glimpse of myself in the mirror. Holy terror. I was as white as the wall behind me.

My eyes were deeply set in two dark circles. I looked like one of those stupid girls in 'B' horror films—the no-talent actresses who trip over a phone cord and scream, "Don't kill me. Are you going to kill me?" as a murderer lifts an eight-foot-long hacksaw above his head.

I peeped out the window. Sunlight was reflecting off a fountain of water shooting from the sprinkler. A rush of energy swept through me. *I want to go home*, I thought. *I want to toss all my clothes in the wash, take a long shower, tie on a bathing suit, slap on baby oil, and lay out in the sun. I want to pour myself a glass of lemonade and feel normal again.* With everyone still passed out, I rose from bed. I tied my hair in a ponytail and left.

That day, as I took the long walk home, I decided I would drink water instead of beer and Schnapps. I would never again balance a cigarette between my fingers. I would throw away the black eyeliner I used to shadow my eyes. I would throw away everything I owned that was black, even my jeans.

White. I loved white. Why didn't I own anything that was white? I would buy white T-shirts, white sweaters, white shoes, white whatever. I wanted to feel clean again, like the Tide commercials. Fresh air. Clean hands.

I never went back to Kim's house again. I'm not sure why or how I did it. Maybe you'd think I watched a TV show or read a magazine that made me change my ways. Nope. I don't know what it was. Something just switched a light on in my head. Maybe there is something inside us—what some people call a voice, and others call willpower. Sometimes I think maybe God had something to do with it.

The biggest, loudest door I ever slammed was when I decided to quit drinking and smoking. I'd have no more hangovers, no more stale smoky smell, no more crummy carnival trips. But for a long while, too, I knew

I would not have many friends. Only one to be exact—one single, faithful friend.

Picture this: It's early October in Minnesota. Crackling leaves cover the ground, but the summer heat is still fighting to hang on a few weeks longer. School is in full swing, and everybody wants to officially kiss the summer good-bye. We throw a huge party in the backyard of somebody's relative's house. The relatives are gone, kids are tapping a keg, and about 20 people are trying to pass me a beer.

"Nope," I say. "I quit."

No one would take "no" for an answer. "Yeah, right, McLinden. You'll drink. You're so full of crap . . . blah, blah, blah."

The comments kept up over the next few weeks. My friends made bets among themselves on when I would crack. When my commitment to quit finally sank in, their rude comments got worse. My friends decided to treat me like an outsider. I became the "milk-

and-cookie" girl. "Hey everyone! Shannon is having a Kool-Aid party. Wanna come?"

No one liked me anymore. And they did a great job of making that absolutely clear to me. The same friends who used to joke with me during class stopped looking in my direction. They purposely ignored me as I tried to stand with them. My pockets were empty at the end of the day, and my phone almost never rang.

Did it hurt? Oh yes. Did I cry? For months. Did I think about drinking again? Yup. Did I give in? No way.

When you know you have made the right decision and you are finally headed on the right path, you feel like nothing can hurt you. The silence of my friends sure couldn't. I knew something they didn't: I would be a happier, better person in the long run. I walked away from drinking, but I also left the whiny, teasing ridicule and jealousy that had surrounded me.

Realizing where you are in your life is not always easy. Picturing where you are going is even more difficult. It finally hit me. I had to sculpt me. I made a list in my journal of qualities I wanted: long hair, no pimples, athletically fit, nice legs, better eating habits (no pizza and fried chicken), brains, pretty, lots of nice friends, great attitude. I could make myself into the person I wanted to be.

Remember I told you I had one friend? That was Amy, my friend from second grade. Over the years, we'd kept up our after-school routine lots of days. We came home together, ate macaroni and cheese, and watched TV until my parents came home. Nothing but the programs changed. We went from *He-Man and the Masters of the Universe* to *Double Dare* to *Little House on the Prairie* to MTV. I always walked her halfway home afterward.

After I quit drinking, Amy never gossiped about me to anyone. In fact, if she heard comments, she defended me. We wrote notes back and forth every day. She called me at night even when she knew none of the other girls would.

Amy saved me from calling it quits on my life. She stayed my friend during the best times and the worst times. She will always be the kind of friend who will dance with me in clouds of bubbles.

chapter seven
jerks

Even though I no longer drank, I decided to go to a New Year's Eve party that year at my friend Jessie's house. There were people there older and younger than me; some I didn't recognize. Everyone but me got drunk. I got sick of listening to pointless, drunken stories, so I went into Jessie's bedroom. I started looking through some photo albums. All at once, the bedroom lights went out and the door clicked shut.

I asked, "Is anyone there?"

No answer. I walked toward the door, thinking someone in the hall had shut out the lights and closed the door, assuming the room was empty.

I was wrong. Someone was in the room. He was over six feet tall and breathing hard. He smelled of stale beer, belches, and cigarettes. He threw me on the bed. One minute later, half my clothes were off. I screamed, kicked hard, flailed my arms, and tried to wrench myself toward the door. *So this is what it's like to be raped.*

For endless minutes, I struggled and screamed. No one burst in to save me.

Where is everyone? The drunken partygoers were outside the door, confused, laughing nervously as they listened.

Someone finally pushed the door open, and the nightmare ended. Sort of. I don't understand what I was thinking. I faintly remember seeing everyone staring at me. I was half naked. Mascara and lipstick were smeared all over my face. My eyes were red and swollen. I should have told everyone what had happened.

I should have left, called the police, and reported that I'd been attacked. *But the police won't believe me. They'll think I was drunk and having a good time. And what would my parents say? They don't even know we have parties like this! Jessie would be dead. The police would arrest everyone who is underage, and everybody here would hate me. They're staring at me already.*

Instead of leaving, I went into the bathroom and cleaned myself up. Then I went back to the party. *Maybe everyone will think we were just joking around in that room, and that I wasn't really attacked.* I actually sat in the same room as this guy. On the same couch. *Maybe if I sit by him and try to talk to him, what happened won't seem so bad. Maybe he didn't mean to hurt me.* I even sat on the same couch cushion. *Maybe we can be friends—or maybe more?*

Yup, we were real good friends. After that, when I walked down the halls at school, this guy's friends would see me and say to him, "There she is! You got her pretty good, huh?"

My dad had warned me about things like this. Why didn't I listen, so that I would have known enough to call the police. So that I would have reported the harassment in the hallways to the principal. So that I would have realized we can grow strong from things that are hard.

That night of the attack, I didn't know how to feel. Somebody dropped me off at home after the party, about two a.m. The temperature outside was around zero, but instead of going inside the house, I waited in the cold until I saw the taillights of the car fade into the night. Then I headed up the icy street to my faithful swing in the park.

When I got to the park entrance, it was blocked by snow piled three feet deep. There was no way I could climb through, so I plopped myself down right there and lay back on the frozen pile. The wrestling match had been long, and I had lost. Every muscle in my body tugged with the strain of the night's events. My wrists stung. A dull ache in the back of my neck snaked up, over my left ear, and made my eye twitch. *I will never be the same me again.*

I breathed in deep. The cold air soothed my chest better than Halls. It felt like the perfect time to cry.

You know, it's funny. Even though each month I'd had a new crush and a new whirlwind of emotion, every relationship I'd had before had soon phased out. I'd always picked up and moved on. I'd never taken a relationship with a boy very far, and no guy had ever made a tremendous impact on me. But this man did. I just wish my "pioneer" of impacts hadn't turned out to be a jerk.

After the attack, I changed almost immediately. You'd think I changed into a withdrawn little girl, a nun who'd avoid sexual intimacies for the rest of my life. Nope. Strange things happen. The monster who left his footprints on my mind took all my innocence and made it so, so easy to find comfort in fast-moving relationships. I lost the voice inside me that told me to slow down. I shocked myself.

For the rest of the year, I did a lot of soul-searching. The snow melted, and I made a lot of trips to the swing. I wrote in my journal every night. One day, I found a poem in a magazine, and a picture of a house I fell in love with. I taped them both in my book. Another day I found a picture of me I really liked. I was sitting on a rock, wearing a blue bathing suit, and the sun was shining just behind my head. I actually thought I looked sort of attractive. I pasted that baby to the front of my book!

I kept adding stuff. Pictures of my friends. Tickets to concerts. Birthday cards. Comic strips that made me laugh. On days when I woke up and thought, *Go back to bed*, I just pulled out that book, reminding myself how I looked and felt in the blue bathing suit, what dreams I had yet to make come true, what goals I had yet to accomplish. My journal became my place of comfort.

Gradually, I returned to the more conservative me I remembered. I quit "scoping out" guys and gave my heart a much-needed vacation. I made a list of New Year's resolutions that will stick for life. One was that I will never drink heavily or date anyone who does.

I began to realize that, someday, a real man would find me. And I remembered what my favorite author, Marianne Williamson, once wrote: "Women are daughters of God, and daughters of God don't brake for jerks."

chapter eight
what it means to be a girl

Did you know that half of all teenage girls diet? I didn't. I thought I was one of the only ones! I've read magazine articles about how being too thin is unhealthy. In an effort to achieve the thin look of supermodels like Kate Moss, some girls are actually killing themselves.

By now, I was trying to "eat better" by just eating salads and breads. I didn't eat breakfast and lunch. Most days, I had my first and only meal at about four in the afternoon. At supper time, I always told my parents I'd already eaten. Somehow my stomach got used to the irregular pattern, and it felt normal to be a little hungry.

Well, the problem came when I added exercise to this freakish eating ritual. I joined a health club, and I'd work out after school and on Saturdays, lifting weights and sprinting around the indoor track. I marked my weight each day on a little chart the club kept on file for me. I kept up this pattern for about three weeks. I lost five pounds!

Then, one Sunday afternoon, about 20 people came over to my house to play a game of snow football. We ran over to the park and rolled around in the snow for hours. Then we went home. After we peeled off our layers of clothing, my friends went to the family room to watch movies. I went to the kitchen to help my mom make hot chocolate. I never made it.

Suddenly, the room started to spin. The floor seemed to move under me. Blackness smothered me as I slid down the wall to the floor. Minutes passed, and some of my friends wondered what had happened to me. Julie came upstairs and found me, slouched in a corner.

My parents rushed me to the emergency room, where a doctor ordered an IV for me. He told my parents (who were in the room where

I was lying), "Your daughter is dehydrated." He said my blood pressure was so low and my heart rate so fast that I was unbelievably close to slipping into a coma. When my parents learned why, they were crushed. Their little girl had starved herself.

Yup. I sure thought I was on a roll at the gym. How about those five pounds! But I had nothing in my body. I had forgotten to eat.

Eating is a life function, just like breathing. If we quit eating enough of the right foods, we die. That's it. I wasn't choosing to die this time. But not eating brought me closer to death than anything else in my life.

It is unreal how easy it is to be dragged into the food war. I had become part of the vicious thinness cycle without really trying. I had no idea. My parents had no idea either. How were they supposed to know? I left for school after they left for work, so they didn't know if I had had breakfast. They let me skip supper since

I told them I had eaten supper after school. I had become an 82-pound skeleton.

My mom and dad had always stocked our kitchen shelves with every kind of food imaginable. They fed my friends and catered my parties. There really wasn't anything I didn't have or anything I could have wanted. Yet food—right there in front of me, offered to me every day by my parents—was the one thing I forgot to take, the one thing I needed most.

Recovery was absolutely horrendous. I had to start slowly. My stomach wasn't used to food. I ate carrots. Then I ate carrots and peas. Then I ate carrots, peas, and rice. Eventually, I added bread, but always with quarts of Gatorade to wash it down. Talk about bad school lunches! School lunches seemed like extravagant feasts compared to my new menus.

Once again, I was a social leper, "the girl who quit eating." People thought I was a freak, that I had done this to myself on purpose. Even my friends didn't understand. How do you convince anyone that you just forgot to eat? No one believed me.

If you think any of the boys I had my eye on gave me the time of day after that, you're wrong. I seemed "screwed up" to them. Why would any guy want to date someone who was trying to kill herself? My eating problem almost killed me off in more ways than one.

My parents made me eat dinner with them after that. It was so funny because my plate was always just covered with food "incorporating all the major food groups." They watched me so closely. So did my friends—the few who were still hanging around. I felt like a guinea pig at lunch. Everybody pretended not to watch me. But they did watch, to make sure I ate. It was unbelievably annoying.

I had to learn a new way to eat. I worked at it. I starting eating about six meals a day—

all small, but nutritious and filling. To make sure my metabolism was up and running, I ate crackers, fruit, vegetables, and cheese all day long. I still avoided anything fried in butter, but I always ate until I was full. It was wonderful. I was never starving.

I don't know what was so appealing about the thin fad. What I learned through that awful experience permanently changed my life. I would rather be able to outrun or out-jump another girl than be the thinnest, weakest girl in a frail body. It took a while, but I did finally bounce back—healthy, strong, and determined—with more "on the ball" than an 82-pound frame that was empty inside.

That summer was one great shopping adventure. Amy and I worked at the wave pool and made a tradition of spending our money every two weeks. On payday. We didn't save a penny, but we did fill our closets with bags and bags of slip dresses, sandals, and T-shirts. Amy and I wore the same size clothes. We could double our wardrobes by shopping together, then picking from each other's closets a couple of times a week.

School started after too short a summer. I quit work, but I still had money rolling in; I always got my parents to lend it to me ("lend" in the "never-see-it-again" sense). Then I was off again on the hunt for great bargains. When the biggest department store in town had a sale, I was the first one there.

"You look like you need some help," this stiff-necked woman announced, stepping out from behind a counter as I was walking through cosmetics. She startled me.

"What?" I asked politely.

"Have you heard about our new sheer foundation? This product is very light, yet it can conceal your skin, which looks like it needs some help," she said with a gigantic smile. "It would really do a lot for your ruddy complexion."

I felt numb. I couldn't believe the words had been directed at me. I wanted to turn my baseball cap backwards and take a swing at her. A hard one. But then it happened. As I stared at her brightly caked face, I made a discovery. *Poor thing. She wakes up each morning believing that, in order to be beautiful, she needs to mask her face in a wash of fake color.*

I didn't swing, and I didn't run away. Something glued my feet to the floor. "Fortunately, I have nothing to hide," I blurted from my chapsticked lips. It was a miracle. On any earlier day, I would have cried with self-pity. For the first time, I did not doubt that I am just fine the way I am. I did not need improvement.

The words of Laura the psychologist finally made a connection with my stubborn brain. She had warned me, long ago, not to "fall fool to a quick fix." Up until then, I had been looking for an external peace—that's a "quick fix." I wanted to make my face prettier, my body leaner, my reputation stronger. I thought peace would come after I was beautiful, thin, and cool. What I figured out is that I needed to find an internal peace—a permanent fix.

Pretty faces get wrinkles. Bodies gain weight. Reputations get killed by one tiny rumor. When you look back over the years, you see that "cool" is something different every minute. I craved something solid.

After my discovery at the makeup counter, I headed to the towers of shelves in every major bookstore in town. I wanted to start reading books to see if anyone out there agreed with me. Sure enough! I found plenty of books that showed people everywhere, of all ages, were dealing with the same issues as me.

The self-help books Laura had recommended weren't so bad after all. Some were so popular I couldn't find copies at the library. At the bookstores where I checked for a copy of *A Revolution Within* (by Gloria Steinem), the last volume had always been sold "just yesterday." The books I read told about people fed up with falling down, people searching for a lift.

I realized lifts wouldn't come from the magazines I'd been reading, like *Seventeen*, *Teen*, and *Young Ms.* I went to a bookstore and compared their covers. The topics they were advertising matched: "How to Flatten Your Tummy in Seven Days." "How to Win a Guy." "Flattering Spring Makeup." "Lose 10 Pounds in 5 Days and Look Great!"

These magazines are telling us to fix ourselves. They tell us to flatten our tummies because they assume our tummies aren't flat. And they assume we *want* them to be. They tell us to wear makeup so that we can look "better." Whatever made these people think we need improvement? What made them think we need a man in our lives? I don't need fashion tips to look fabulous, and I don't need or want to lose 10 pounds.

Besides, the articles are so misleading. You can't flatten your tummy in seven days. Men can't be won. (Together, you either like each other or you don't.) You won't look fabulous in a spring fashion unless you already look exactly like the woman modeling it. And she's five-foot-nine inches tall and weighs 100 pounds.

I decided to become so strong, emotionally, that someone like the woman at the makeup counter could not matter to me. She could point-blank tell me I was ugly. And I'd laugh. "Your opinion is of no concern to me," I could say. "Only one thing matters to me. I am a good person with potential to be more amazing than you could ever imagine."

I began to use this speech (or versions of it) on a great many people. Every time I got better at it. And every time I reminded myself of the truth. No one can make me feel inferior unless I let them. And I will never give my consent.

Nothing on the outside matters. There are gorgeous women everywhere who show no care for others. They lose their beauty every time they open their mouths. I won't accept any lies—only the truth. Being happy as a female does not require big boobs, a tiny waist, and makeup to cover flaws. The only flaw we will ever have is believing that anything on the outside matters. Yeah, it seemed like the outside was all that mattered to my friends and to the boys in school. But I wouldn't let it matter to me. I would leave the beauty treadmill to the fad junkies.

I would leave the thinness treadmill to them, too. We can successfully achieve our goal of being thin—and get a ticket to heaven to boot! What a deal, huh? I had almost bought my own ticket to heaven. I hadn't even realized I was at risk.

I began to make it a point to talk with people who would share their wisdom with me—teachers, school counselors, women in grocery store lines, travelers sitting beside me on the bus, even psychologists. Which brings me to one of the most shocking things I discovered: Only five percent of people in the *world* look like the models and actors in the media.

Obviously, the odds of looking like a model are really low. But because the media is so much a part of our lives, we feel like a really small group of imperfect fish in a sea of normal fish. In reality, we are the normal fish, bombarded with images of a few fish who are not the norm. On the average, teens watch 21 hours of TV a week. That is 21 hours of receiving messages telling us lies.

I started to see that the media has convinced millions of men and women that mega-made-up faces and too-thin frames are in. There are men wandering the streets looking for women who look like supermodels Kate Moss or Cindy Crawford. Even the guys in my school searched endlessly. Good luck, guys! And there are even more women doing anything possible to look like those models so they can win those men.

I wanted to find out if I could ever look like those models. I asked someone in science research. What do you know! A person like me *cannot* physically look like Kate Moss and still be healthy. The thin ideal is an ideal that can't be reached. Our culture has developed a standard of beauty that can't be obtained. It isn't natural. One psychologist told me that's why girls end up doing unnatural things to themselves.

Little by little, I was uncovering peace in my life. I searched and searched for reasons to be proud to be me. As I found them, I was able to look in a mirror and not cry. I learned not to be obsessed with changing from the outside in. Instead, I focused on transforming from the inside out. *Thank you, Laura.* I was relearning what it means to be a girl.

chapter nine
fixing the family

By now some of my old friends (most of the girls, surprisingly) accepted the fact that I didn't drink; they even thought what I stood for was pretty cool. I volunteered to become their sober cab.

It was a lot of responsibility—steering a car full of raving females to parties and home again. I had to make sure every one of them—whether sober, tipsy, or slippery drunk—arrived back on her own doorstep with everything intact. I loved it. My friends trusted me with their lives. Just knowing that made me feel respected, important. In fact, I felt pretty good about myself. *Imagine that! I never thought I'd feel good about anything!*

The next big job I had was to fix a relationship I had destroyed—my relationship with my family. It hadn't taken me long to ruin my family's *Leave It to Beaver* life. Of course, at the time, I wouldn't have admitted that I ruined it.

Remember my antics of not talking to my parents? They were smart. They decided to play my game. If I wouldn't talk to them, they would do the same to me. When I needed to talk, or when I just had a simple question ("What's for dinner?"), they were unresponsive.

I felt terrible. I thought my parents had given up on me. They weren't supposed to do that. My outbreaks were no fun if my parents could treat me the way I treated them. Screaming at them was *really* not fun if they didn't seem to care.

Oddly enough, though, it was my brother who gave me the biggest reality check. He sat me down one day. "Shannon, I don't know what Mom and Dad did to you to make you hate them," he said. "They want you to be part of their lives. I bet they'd do anything to have you speak normally to them again. Please don't let anything stupid tear down the bridge

between you so you can never meet halfway."
Yes, believe it or not: The same brother who
put me in a box and threw me down a flight of
stairs said something this brilliant.

Shortly after, I read part of a book that
helped put things even more in perspective.
The book explained parents like this: Two
people met and loved each other. They may
have loved each other for one night, or for
years. But in one moment, you became a life
in your mother's womb. She sat at night with
her hand on her belly, feeling you kick. She
thought about the places she'd take you, about
all she wanted to buy you, about everything
you would be as an adult. After months of
anticipation, after hours in a hospital in much
pain, she gave birth to you—a little seven-
pound creature. You didn't pop out waving an
instruction manual on babies in your parents'
faces. Even so, they managed to show you
how to walk, talk, use a toilet. Most of the

fundamentals (not all) that gradually made you who you are (good and bad) came from the people who raised you.

It was easy for me to look at my parents and claim: "Everything is their fault. I hate them." But they were two people who could only do their best. They deserved a break. A big break. They didn't know what school was like. I had to tell them. They didn't know what the fashions were. I had to show them. They didn't know I hated it when they reminded me of my responsibilities. I had to let them know how I felt. What they did not know was not their fault.

I tried to do something the book suggested. I turned the tables on myself. I imagined that I had switched roles with my parents. Instead of picturing myself hiding things from them, screaming at them, ignoring them, I tried to imagine myself as the parent type. Here's how the picture looked:

I come home from school. My mom is lying on the couch watching MTV. I say, "Hey, Mom. What's up? What are you doin'?"

She looks up. No answer. I see her mumble, but hear no words. "I'm sorry, I can't hear you," I tell her. "What did you say?"

"I'm doing nothing, okay? God!!!" Mom gets up, goes to her room, and slams the door. I hear her scream from behind her door, "I hate you!"

Whoa. What was that? Little do I know, Mom is pissed because I did not make my bed. The kitchen sink is full of dishes from breakfast. And some ladies at work made fun of her new dress. She wants to be alone. The last person she wants to deal with is me.

How did I feel when I imagined this scene? Like my mom had slapped me in the face! It's funny. I'd never seen how my own outbursts must appear. I'd been thinking, *She's just my mom, you know? She's annoying.* So I let her have it. *She can handle it.*

Wrong. Her only daughter, a person she raised and loves, says, "I hate you." The daughter shuts her out and wants to be alone. That would make you feel pretty empty, wouldn't it?

We started to work things out, my parents and I. The first thing I did was to drop the bomb. I told them about my life. I told them that many times I'd taken liquor from their wine cabinet. I told them that I'd skipped school. I told them that if they had to live through my days, they wouldn't just skip school—they'd quit.

You know what was shocking? They listened. What a relief it was having them know I am not perfect, nor ever will be. It was almost better that way. I knew they wouldn't be shocked the next time I did something wrong.

After that, I still felt like screaming "I hate you!" sometimes. Sometimes I felt like crying. Sometimes I felt like saying "I love you." I didn't say that; I'm still working up to it. But at least my parents and I began to rebuild the bridge that let us meet halfway—a bridge that for too long a time had fallen into ruin.

chapter ten
princes

After the New Year's Eve party when I was attacked, it took me a long time to realize the most important fact. That guy hurt my body, but that was all. Bruises go away. Cuts heal. He never touched my mind or stole my heart. My soul is fully intact.

In fact, believe it or not, he helped me. I said I made a New Year's resolution that I would never drink heavily or date a guy who did. Well, you can bet that, as my high school years went by, I affirmed that resolution a hundred times.

Sex is easy. It's a physical act—that's all. It can happen between two strangers, even when one is not willing. I want more from guys than just sex. After that New Year's Eve, I began to look at guys in a whole new way. I began to look for a guy with sensitivity—caring, helpful, friendly, and optimistic.

We should never lower our expectations when dealing with men. We should make them earn our hearts, and wait to be invited into our personal space. I became picky, not because I'm "tight," but because I'm an above-average girl seeking an above-average guy. And every one of us is awesome in a unique way. Competition for our companionship should be intense.

I also wanted a guy with brains. In eighth grade, some of the guys teased me by calling me a "nerd." I figured out that if I want a man who is smart, he will probably want someone who is smart too. I'm not necessarily talking about "book smart," but "people smart." He'd respect me because I take care of my body and my mind. Just as much, I wanted a guy who would be friends before partners. A guy with a character like Amy's—someone to make bubbles with. Someone to watch movies, build tree forts, and dream with. A guy who would laugh with me in the good times, and cry with me in the bad.

And guess what? In high school, I started meeting guys who fit most of those great qualities. I was introduced to a football player named Jon. He swept me into the clouds with such refreshing beliefs as "no sex before marriage." We went together for two years. And then I was privileged to meet Steve, who became one of my best friends after we'd dated and broken up in an intense, painful ending.

As a couple, Jon and I—or Steve and I— never could have been happy together forever. But by attempting a relationship with them, I learned about how to truly love someone. I learned by being so bad at attempting! Without them, I never would have experienced a gentle hand to hold. I wouldn't have had a gigantic hug good-bye. I treasured the fragments of puppy love they gave me, and kept the fragments as standards against which to measure the men in my future.

A rude or vulgar man could look like Brad Pitt, and no one could pay me to marry the fool. I saw that the greatest people in the world—in history, and in everyday life—make a positive difference in the lives of others not because they have a beautiful smile or thousands of friends or a new Porsche, but because their hearts are in the right place. They help others put their hearts in the right place, too.

A year after I graduated from high school, my friend Dan threw a party. I went, just for a little while. All my middle school friends were there, even friends who had gone on to different high schools.

As I was leaving the party, a man walked up to me. He was Mike—that good-looking guy I'd once wanted to date. He leaned over with a big smile that showed he was still just as conceited as he'd been then. "Wow, Shannon," he yelled over the thump of music. "You look great! Would you want to go out sometime?"

"What did you say?" I asked him, reveling in the moment. "I can't hear you!"

He shouted again. "Would you want to go out sometime?"

"No," I said with my own big smile. "But thanks!" What a night. I remember skipping back to my car in the freezing cold, driving home, and slipping into my pajamas. *The Princess Bride* was playing on HBO. I love the hero, Wesley, with his beautiful eyes and kind ways. He searches for the woman he truly loves, and when he finds her, he always tells her, "As you wish." He's a prince.

chapter eleven
getting my life back

Some people say, "There's always a chance." I have never agreed—not where happiness is concerned. There's always a chance with weather? Yes. Cards? Maybe. Happiness? No way. The only time chance is involved with your own happiness is when you have done nothing to create it.

Unfortunately, this took me years to understand. I wasn't happy because I *chose* not to be happy. Everyone gets a bad perm sometime, loses a boyfriend, or gets left out. The problem is that some people dwell on the failures. I did for a long time.

I left myself completely open for chance to barrel me over. Was there a chance I would be sad? Yup. Was there a chance I would cry and carry on about how terrible life can be? You bet. Was there a chance I'd want to die? Oh yes. Who wouldn't! Because I never created my own happiness.

I started to create happiness when I decided

I had to sculpt me. Remember the list of qualities I wanted (long hair, no pimples, athletically fit, nice legs, better eating habits, brains, pretty, nice friends, great attitude)? By the end of high school, I had check marks next to all those goals.

I grew my short, curly hair down to the middle of my back. To clear up my pimples, I experimented with all kinds of face soaps and acne products. (Clinique helped. So did Clearasil, Neutrogena, and my favorite, Cetaphil soap.)

Athletically fit was tough. Heck, in eighth grade, I couldn't even run a complete circle around my block. I started exercising at a health club, yes. But I learned that to exercise, I also needed to eat. I trained my brain to crave good food. I also noticed that my workouts didn't always work out. I'd sprint a lap. Socialize. Do five leg presses. Socialize. That pattern wasn't making me athletically fit.

So I started jogging through my neighborhood. I started with a short distance, adding the length of one house at a time to my jog as time went by. I worked my way up to five miles a day. Before long I had muscle I could see when I looked in the mirror! Muscle in my arms, muscle in my legs. Ha! If I'd seen that years ago, I would have fainted.

As for eating habits, soon after I started eating right I looked more like my ideal than I had when I was starving myself. I still eat about six filling meals a day of crackers, fruit, vegetables, and cheese. I get to enjoy that satisfied, lazy feeling of eating until I'm stuffed. And amazingly, the rolls of "fat" I saw on myself in eighth grade have gradually, but healthily, been smoothed from my skin. (Sounds like a commercial, huh?) My face has more color, my hair has more shine, my nails are stronger. I look pretty good! And I have unlimited energy and a skip in my step to boot.

I already had brains when I made the list. I think I added brains just to make sure I stayed smart. I focused on being a good person. But I also studied hard, preparing myself for my goal—college. I ignored the guys at school who teased me about being a "nerd" for getting good grades. In the end I didn't care what the slackers thought of me; I wasn't attracted to slackers. My man would be intelligent and caring.

Nice friends and a great attitude—the last two things on my list—supported each other. I quit spending time with anyone who did not make me feel good about being who I was. Why put myself through the torture? It was hard, I will admit. Popularity was always so important to me. But I decided, finally, to stay on the out. When I quit trying to be like my friends, it took so much pressure and hurt off me. I wore the clothes I thought looked good on me and developed my own quirky laugh. I got off the treadmill I'd been spinning on, trying to keep up with the trends.

When I did that, I really felt for the first time like I had confidence. And on days when the cute boy I liked ignored me, I told myself over and over, *Someday this boy and other boys will see in me something wonderful and different from the rest.*

Instead, I made and kept more friends like my friend Amy, who always supported me and my dreams. I built an optimistic attitude by hanging around her and other people who built me up. I stopped letting anyone tell me that some of my dreams had "never been done and couldn't be done," or that someone like me couldn't get where I wanted to go. I turned my back on those people, kept going toward my goal, and sent them a postcard when I got there.

Yes, high school brought a lot of positive changes, and I added them all to my journal. My senior year I was elected president of the student body. I was voted to Spring Royalty Court. The highest honor I have ever received was being voted "Most Likely to Succeed." I was accepted to the universities I applied to. I ended up with my brother, Scott, at Texas Christian University (TCU).

I even received some scholarships to TCU. I was never a straight-A student in high school. I just worked hard and tried to be well rounded. (Straight-A students didn't get the local scholarships I received. Just me—your everyday, hardworking student!) I figured out that we need to redefine what smart is. My brother teaches great crash courses for mathematical dummies. Amy takes computers apart and puts them together again. I give pretty good love advice. Zach fixes car engines. Each of us at one time said, "I'm so dumb."

But we were never dumb. We are all smart in a different way. And each of us deserves a pat on the back. Everyone I know has heard about my friends' accomplishments from me first.

In college, I gave up my social life for three years to study extremely hard. I earned my bachelor's degree a year early, and I was accepted into TCU's master's program in business administration. I'm at TCU as I write this book—one of the youngest students ever enrolled in the program.

I kept being picky about men. I refused to feel bad about saying no to sex. If ever a guy makes fun of me for saying no, I've got a speech ready for him. "Look buddy," I'll tell him, "I'm sorry to bring you down from your throne, but when and if I have sex with a man, he will be someone who far surpassses the extraordinary. You are not him."

At last, one day at TCU, I looked up from a paper I was reading and met the warm eyes of a towering, dark man. He was Middle Eastern, his name was Hani, and we quickly became best friends. For weeks we palled around, eating lunch together and watching every new movie that hit the screens. Several nights we just sat on the floor of my apartment and talked about the worst and best times of our lives.

If we had just remained best friends, I would have been the happiest person alive. But one evening, he drove us to a restaurant along a cobblestone street where lights brightened the trees like Christmas. At a candlelit table, Hani leaned toward me, squeezed my hand, and asked if he could kiss me. I knew then, as I looked into his gentle eyes, that I had found a prince.

It's hard to struggle against the flow with just a few people on your side. But do you know what the rewards have been for me? Joy. Mornings when I actually wake up and smile. Nights when I don't cry. Days when I have the enthusiasm to carry out my dreams. Friends who support me and help me. Life. I got my life back. I found the me I always knew I had inside.

chapter twelve
a peaceful world

So many girls walk around dead on their feet. I was dead on mine. Some of my best friends were dead on theirs. But along the way, we realized that the world was filling our heads with craziness. It was time to start rejecting those thoughts.

It's easy to feel alone in the struggle to feel happy. Know this: You are not alone—even if you feel at times as though you can't go on. Researchers say that one in four adolescents is at risk of suicide each year. The next time you're in class, count down to the fourth person in your row of desks. Then count another four. Then another. There are probably eight or nine people in that classroom who feel the way I did. The way you may feel sometimes. Multiply the people in your classroom by the number of classrooms in the world. Alone? Far from it.

We can find the tools and the strength to tear down the lies. Lies like the ones we are told on TV: If you don't look like this, you are ugly. If you don't weigh this, you are fat. If you can't solve this, you are stupid. If you don't smoke this or drink that, you are nobody. Looks don't matter that much. Being happy as a female does not require "fixing" our flaws. The only flaw we will ever have is believing that the outside matters.

In adult life, popularity starts to mean nothing to everybody. Ten years after middle school, almost everyone is working or married. I can tell you that I don't care what birthday parties I go to. Some of the people who were rude to me in middle school have become people I don't care to see today. The only opinions I care about are those of the people I love and respect.

You need to live your dreams. To do that, you need to be strong. Don't let anyone make you feel inferior. People can say anything they choose, but they can only make you feel inferior if you let them. Stand up for yourself. Stand up with the truth. You have the tools and the strength to tear down lies. That's why I've told my story to you—so you will know what you may face before you get there.

If you read from the books, listen to the stories, search through your own life, and question all of the crap the world hands to you, you will be made strong. And afterwards, you can throw a cherry on top and call it a day.

Seven years ago, I sported black clothes and partied at friends' houses where I would get so drunk I would fall asleep hunched over a toilet with strings of my hair dangling in the water. I cried about how hard my life was, and how I couldn't believe I had so many problems. My life, my world, felt as hollow as the bowl. So I stepped out into a busy, unlit street. I almost walked myself right out of my life. What really saved me was my faith that nothing ever remains the same—not even my dreary days.

I am strong, and I am finally happy. All of us who struggle in pain and recover have an advantage forever. Seven days, or seven years, after we break through the dark, we are stronger than ever before. Some people suffer a midlife crisis. Not us. Our crisis is preadult. We can survive to live in a peaceful world. And our midlives will be bliss. Pure bliss.

reader's discussion guide

Questions for Discussion

1. The poem on page 11 was written by Shannon when she was 12 to herself as an adult. What does this poem say to you?

2. As a reflection of herself, Shannon only wore dark clothes. What kinds of things do people you know do or wear to reveal how they feel about themselves to the world?

3. Shannon writes about being depressed: "My girlfriends were sort of aware of how I felt. But like most girls our age, they didn't seem to want anyone but themselves to get attention. Rather than sympathize with me, they shrugged me off and kept the attention on themselves" (14–15). How do you think people your age react to their friends and acquaintances being depressed?

4. "People would ask me, 'What's wrong?' 'Nothing,' I'd say. I should have said, 'Everything. I'm depressed.' Although the word *depressed* doesn't quite wrap up how I felt. I don't think there are words for that. My feelings were more like a long moan with jumbles of letters thrown in here and there. *UUUhhpffftgguuuughstfmoh*. Yeah, that's better" (14). Have you ever felt that you didn't have the right words to describe your feelings? Did this keep you from talking about your feelings? If you can find (or create) the exact right words to describe the feelings, do you think it helps you and others to understand the feelings or make the situation better?

5. Shannon went to a swing in a park by her house at night when she was troubled. When you have problems, what do you do? Who do you go to for sharing and advice?

6. What does "being a good friend" mean to you? What kinds of things do you do for others as a "good friend"?

7. Shannon describes but can't explain why her relationship with her parents deteriorated. "One morning I woke up, looked at my mom, and thought, *Ugh. I don't want to talk to her.* . . . There was always a different story for my anger. A lot of times the story didn't make sense. The bottom line was, I always said I hated [my parents]" (18–19). Can you relate to this experience of suddenly changing how you see your family but not understanding why? Have you seen this happen between other family members?

8. Shannon lists aspects of her appearance that she obsessed over: curly brown hair, weight/chubby thighs, dimples, freckles,

and weird-shaped toenails. She felt anyone looking at her was "staring at my ugly face or my screwed-up hair" (22). What do you think of this list of "flaws"? What do you think of her reaction to people looking at her?

9. Shannon uses an interesting metaphor to try to explain her feelings: "Things all around just never seemed to go my way. And every one of those things piled in my mind like junk stuffed in a closet, just waiting for the door to open so it could tumble out in a ferocious wave" (24–25). Do you have strategies to keep the junk from piling up in your mind? Shannon's reaction to the "door" of her "closet" bursting open was a suicide attempt. What other reactions do you think people have to their minds getting too full of junk and their "closet doors" bursting open?

10. "Alcohol made it easier for me to talk to people about my feelings," (25) Shannon says. What other experiences or things do people seek out to help them talk about their feelings? Can you divide your list into good and bad ways of opening up?

11. "*Why is my life so hard,* I wondered. *I'm pretty good looking, smart, outgoing, even funny sometimes. I know I am all these things, but I don't feel like I'm any of them*" (27). What is the difference between knowing something about yourself and feeling that you are actually good looking, smart, and funny? How does a person move from "knowing" something to "feeling" something?

12. This quote from Marianne Williamson was important to Shannon in understanding her own thoughts and behavior: "We just get tired, or we get reborn, when we have

suffered so much that we have started to die" (13). What does this quote mean to you?

13. Do you think it's true, as Shannon says, that most girls are at some point attracted to "no-mannered, nonshowering, foul-mouthed, or uncaring guys" (31)—in other words, a guy who doesn't show them much consideration? Do you think boys believe this to be true?

14. Shannon asks girls and women, "Why is it we feel like we are nothing without a boy in our lives?" (37) What do you think?

15. Shannon describes dressing and acting like the girls that she felt were the most popular with the guys: "For a while, I really thought my plan was going to work. I'd look and feel just like them. But I

never got more than a temporary feeling of 'okayness'" (41). Why do you think this strategy didn't work? Have you ever attempted to imitate someone? Is it always bad to imitate?

16. We know when Shannon met Laura, the psychologist, Shannon hated her and only went to three sessions of therapy. However, she mentions Laura's advice a few times later in the book. How do you think she felt about Laura later on? How do you think as an adult Shannon looks back on the experience of therapy during middle school?

17. Shannon mentions some of the social groups she perceived at her school: geeks, headbangers, freaks, and the wild crowd. She calls herself a floater and discusses changing her behavior depending on the

group she was with. She says, "I could fit in everywhere. Yet really I fit in nowhere, because I could never be the real me" (48). What groups do you see at your school? Are some people floaters? Do you think that identifying with a group changes people's behavior? Is it bad to be influenced by friends? How can you "be the real me" and still be close to your friends?

18. Shannon charts her popularity score each day by the number of people by her locker, how many people sit with her at lunch, how many notes she receives, and how many phone calls she gets after school. What other ways do people judge how popular they are? Shannon says, "For a long time I had so many friends that I couldn't even count them. Yet I'd never been so lonely or confused" (51). Do you think anyone you know feels as Shannon did?

19. Shannon says she envied "people who were shy or quiet . . . they were so removed from the action . . . that to them middle school was just like summer camp" (51). Do you think it's true that the "middle-school wallflowers" are better off? Do you think they don't feel the same social pressures as other people?

20. At the end of the chapter "Bad Crowds," in which Shannon describes the fights, drinking, and drug use of her "bad crowd," she realizes her mom knows some of what she's been doing: "I reeked—of too much smoke, alcohol, anger, recklessness, dirt, lying, shame, and hurt" (77). What is the connection between each of the things in that list?

21. Shannon says she's not sure why or how she decided to quit drinking and smoking. Why do you think she decided this?

22. Do you think someone in your school or social circle would be made fun of for a decision to quit drinking or smoking? Why or why not?

23. Shannon recounts her experience of being sexually assaulted at a party and says the result was that it "made it so, so easy to find comfort in fast-moving relationships. I lost the voice inside me that told me to slow down. I shocked myself" (91–92). Why do you think she reacted in this way?

24. Why do you think Shannon's resolution to be happier and "eat better" (95) led to an eating disorder? Do you think it's common that our resolutions to improve our lives can lead to more unhappiness? Do you think Shannon should have had different resolutions?

25. What do you think of the distinction Shannon discovered between "external peace" and "internal peace"? (103) What observations do you have about magazines and other media aimed at you?

26. What do you think Shannon means when she says "I was relearning what it means to be a girl" (109)? What do you think it means to be a girl or a guy?

27. When Shannon starts thinking about trying to fix her relationship with her family, she realizes she assumed her parents could "*handle it*" (116) when she yelled at them or ignored them. What have you thought that your family can handle even if you might realize they don't really deserve it?

28. Shannon explains her ultimate revelation by saying, "I wasn't happy because I *chose*

not to be happy" (125). Do you agree that happiness or unhappiness is a choice independent of what happens to you in life?

29. What do you think are the top ten problems affecting people your age today?

30. Shannon grew up in the 1990s. How has life changed for people your age? What things are the same?

Recommended Books

Angelou, Maya. *Wouldn't Take Nothing for My Journey Now*. New York: Random House, 1993.

Canfield, Jack. *Chicken Soup for the Teenage Soul: The Real Deal Challenges: Stories about Disses, Losses, Messes, Stresses, and More*. Deerfield Beach, FL: HCI Teens, 2006.

Fulghum, Robert. *All I Really Need to Know I Learned in Kindergarten*. New York: Ivy Books, 1986.

Gantos, Jack. *Hole in My Life*. New York: Farrar, Straus and Giroux, 2002.

Gourley, Catherine. *Ms. and the Material Girl: Perceptions of Women from the 1970s through the 1990s*. Minneapolis: Twenty-First Century Books, 2008.

Grealy, Lucile. *Autobiography of a Face*. New York: Houghton Mifflin Company, 1994.

Gwartney, Debra. *Live Through This: A Mother's Memoir of Runaway Daughters and Reclaimed Love*. Boston: Houghton Mifflin Harcourt, 2009.

Helmstetter, Shad. *What to Say When You Talk to Yourself.* New York: MFJ Books, 1996.

Hyde, Margaret O., and Elizabeth H. Forsyth. *Stress 101: An Overview for Teens*. Minneapolis: Twenty-First Century Books, 2008.

Jansen, Hanna. *Over a Thousand Hills I Walk with You*. Minneapolis: Carolrhoda Books, 2006.

Louden, Jennifer. *The Woman's Comfort Book*. San Francisco: Harper San Francisco, 1992.

Matthews, Andrew. *Being Happy!* Los Angeles: Price Stern Sloan, 1990.

Moragne, Wendy. *Depression*. Minneapolis: Twenty-First Century Books, 2001.

Murphy, Wendy. *Weight and Health*. Minneapolis: Twenty-First Century Books, 2008.

Myers, Walter Dean. *Bad Boy: A Memoir*. New York: HarperCollins Publishers, 2001.

Pipher, Mary. *Reviving Ophelia*. New York: Ballantine Books, 1994.

Ray, Veronica. *Choosing Happiness*. New York: HarperCollins Publishers, 1990.

Runyon, Brent. *The Burn Journals*. New York: Alfred A. Knopf, 2004.

Williamson, Marianne. *A Return to Love*. New York: HarperPerennial, 1993.

———. *A Woman's Worth*. New York: Ballantine Books, 1993.

Wurtzel, Elizabeth. *Prozac Nation*. New York: Riverhead Books, 1994.

Recommended Magazines and Websites

All about Us
Shannon McLinden's website
http://www.allaboutus.com

GirlsHealth
http://www.girlshealth.gov

Girl Zone
http://www.girlzone.com

New Moon
P.O. Box 3587
Duluth, MN 55803
http://www.newmoon.org

Teen Growth
11274 West Hillsborough Avenue
Tampa, FL 33635
http://www.teengrowth.com

Teen Mental Health
http://www.teenmentalhealth.org/

TeensHealth
http://kidshealth.org/teen

Teen Voices
P.O. Box 120-027
Boston, MA 02112
http://www.teenvoices.com

About the Author

 Shannon McLinden graduated in 1998 with her MBA from Texas Christian University. For several years, she traveled the country visiting schools and sharing her motivational message with teens. Today she resides in Frisco, Texas, with her husband, Hani, her "prince" in the book *The Me Nobody Knew*. Shannon is the founder of several companies including the luxury bath and body line, FarmHouse Fresh®, and an innovative footwear accessories brand, Summer Soles®. She spends most of her time dreaming, designing, and bringing her new ideas to life through her work with these two burgeoning brands.